What P(
abo

MW00626763

The Truth about Being an Extra

Jo Kelly has put together an easy to read and user friendly tool to get your foot in the door in the TV/film business. Unfortunately, there are individuals out there looking to take advantage of those trying to "break in." The Truth about Being an Extra will help you steer clear of those unnecessary pitfalls. If you've always dreamed about working in TV and/or film, but you don't have an uncle who's a producer and you have no idea how to get started, Jo's meticulously organized book is essential in helping you make that dream become a reality.

– Jayme Petrille, Writer

I am so impressed with how much Jo cares about the trials, errors, careers and success of background performers. She has a way of distilling her vast experience and research in an easy to follow manual that allows the novice and the seasoned performer as well to stay on top of their career choice. Information is key and Jo gives it freely and expertly.

– Elisabeth Noone, Actress/Voice Over Coach

(This book) is most informative, to the point and professional. I was glad I could contribute some of my knowledge, after the many years of trials and tribulations working in the business.

– Suzanne Covington, SAG and AFTRA Actress

Jo Kelly is a gift to the entertainment industry! Many will have a smoother ride and fewer heartbreaks because Jo Kelly has been kind enough to share her wealth of wisdom, experiences ... good, bad and indifferent ... with the world. What a lady!

– Janice Smallwood-McKenzie,
The Networking Coach

When I first met Jo Kelly, she told me about her quest to take the mystery out of the movie industry. I wondered how she was going to share that information. She was so full of experience in the movie industry, that I would learn more each time I talked with her.

Her seminar was several hours long and very worthwhile, but I wondered how she would take that information to everyone who would want to be a background actor (extra)? The answer was to write a book. Make it full of information, suggestions, tips and referrals. She did just that ... and filled it with her personality, too. This book is Jo and Jo is about this industry. If you have ever wanted to know more about being an extra, you need to read this book at least twice. There is that much great information between the covers.

– Jack Nichols, President, J. Lloyd and Associates

The Truth about Being an Extra

How to Become a Good Background Actor

By Jo Kelly

August II Productions

The Truth About Being an Extra:
How to Become a Good Background Actor

Published by: August II Productions
Cover Design: Michael Wheary, Foresight Enterprises
Interior Production: Wordpix Solutions
Printed and Bound in the United States of America

Every effort was made to present information in this book accurately, to the best of our knowledge, based on information from sources believed to be reliable and information current at the time of the writing of this book.

ISBN 0-9771878-0-2
ISBN 978-0-9771878-0-5

For information about sales, to contact the author or to request Cataloging-in-Publication information, please contact the Publisher:

August II Productions
19315 Champion Lane
Huntington Beach, CA 92648

www.jkelly4extras.com

Table of Contents

1 Action! Getting Started.................................. 1

2 Casting Agencies 7

3 Casting Children 15

4 Calling Services 25

5 Talent Agencies 31

6 The Good, the Bad & the Ugly 35

7 The First Day 41

8 On the Set Pointers 45

9 Screen Actors Guild 53

10 Wardrobe 57

11 Production Studios.................................. 61

12 Access for the Disabled 67

13 Photography 71

14 Movie Cars 75

15 The Business of Background Acting 79

16 Soap Operas 83

It's a Wrap 89

Glossary 91

Sources & Resources 99

Cutaways 103

Index 105

Dedication

This book is dedicated to my guardian angel, Jack Kelly, to my daughter, Nicole Kelly Garner for all her guidance, and to Bill for his everlasting patience.

Acknowledgments

I'd like to thank Toastmasters International, without which this book would never have been written. When I walked into the Lido Isle Master Toasters meeting in 2002, I was terrified. Within my first year in the club, I completed ten speeches and earned the CTM (Competent Toastmaster) designation. By the end of three years, the inspiration to produce my "How to Get Cast as an Extra" seminars materialized, and I had gained the experience of giving presentations and competing in speech contests and had begun developing the concept for this book. I truly appreciate all the great Toastmasters members who supported my learning efforts, especially Dave Cates, who wrote my marketing plan.

High on my appreciation list is the wonderful Janice Smallwood McKenzie, networking coach and author of *The 101 Commandments of Networking: Common Sense but Not Common Practice.* We met at a Learning Annex public speaking class. During a break, Janice asked me about my work in background acting, and she inquired, pointedly, "So why aren't you teaching?" Stunned at the question, I stammered, "Well, I never thought about it." Janice planted a seed that received immediate nurturing, took root and blossomed into my seminars and, eventually, this book. Janice's web site: www.101NetworkingCommandments.com.

Jayme Petrille and I struck up a conversation in a restaurant in New York City, which led to my sharing that I worked as a non-union extra and that my goal was to get three vouchers so I could join the Screen Actors Guild. A writer for television sitcoms, Jayme took the photo I later sent to him and helped me qualify for SAG. I'll never forget the kindness of this stranger who followed through. The continuing friendship with Jayme and his wife, Silvia, is a rewarding one.

Before I began to envision my website, I interviewed several web design firms. But my friend Blanche Katz suggested I talk with Peggi Ridgway, who owns a web services firm (www.Wordpix.com). I am grateful for that recommendation. Peggi does more than web design. She's a professional writer and published author who really showed me the ropes about creating both my website and my book. And then she introduced me to publicity and promotional opportunities online and in the real world, for the website and the book. Peggi's book, *Successful Website Marketing,* is my regular companion.

My beautiful daughter, Nicole, played an essential role in the writing and production of this book. Nicole, a very successful TV producer and writer on the East Coast, can now add editing to her tools of the trade. She continues to be my strength and she always encourages me and helps me learn. Nicole has guided me, helped me to write this book and she walked me through many situations when I didn't have a clue how to continue. Her good friend, and now mine, Elisabeth Noone, an actress and voice over performer, was also a great help to me in writing the book. Elisabeth also teaches acting workshops. www.ElisabethNoone.com.

As a member of the Speakers Bureau, I met a wonderful man named Victor Broski who spent endless hours coaching me. Victor gave me many valuable tips on my speeches for contests that I entered and I am eternally grateful. More about Victor at www.The SpeechPro.com.

Another wonderful man I met at Speakers Bureau was Jack Nichols, who mentored me, even when I didn't realize I was being mentored. Jack gave me tips on speech contests, reviewed my Toastmaster Live On Air tapes and gave me sage advice in all areas of speaking, that one could only get from a professional such as Jack Nichols.

So much love has gone into this book. I've written this book on behalf of all the new people who will enter the background actors industry with high hopes and big dreams. I know that, with the information in this book, you can avoid the pitfalls and scams, save yourself from heartbreak and soar to success beyond your wildest imagination.

My love and thanks to you all,
Jo Kelly – September 2005

From the Author

I'm happy to welcome you to *The Truth about Being an Extra,* because it means the world to me to help you avoid making mistakes and learn, along the way, some cool little techniques for easily working your way up the acting ladder of success.

I wrote this book in order to produce a creative, informative, helpful and entertaining book with honesty and integrity. It's easy to get registered with casting agencies. This book helps you discover reputable, legitimate agencies and will save you time and money. More importantly, it will help you avoid disappointments, pitfalls and scams.

All you ever need to know to succeed as an "extra" in the entertainment industry is in your hands. Literally, in your hands at this moment as you hold and read this book. Within these pages you'll learn the tips, the shortcuts and the do's and don't's about succeeding as a background actor in movies, television and commercials. How successful you become, how often you are called, how often you work, how much money you make and how much fun you have are all up to you. Let me be your guide.

The road to becoming a background actor is heavily traveled. Like many roads we travel in life, there are sharp turns. With the guidance of this book, you will also know when to slow down. There are also unexpected bumps in the road that I'll help you to avoid. As your guide, I will help make your ride smoother and safer, simply because I know the road. I've traveled it many times.

In fact, that's how my seminars and this book came about. I did not have the guidance I'm offering you. If only I'd had the luxury and comfort of a trusted friend to walk the road of background acting with me. With such a friend, I wouldn't have made so many mistakes! However, I made them. And I learned. Now I want to help you avoid making mistakes and wasting your money, time and dreams on scams and false promises.

In this book, you'll find reputable casting agencies in Los Angeles (Hollywood), along with information on how to register with them. Best of all, you will learn how to start working the very next day. I'll give you the tools to get started and will help you prepare yourself for work. I'll show you the steps for joining Screen Actors Guild (SAG) (which will double your pay and provide you with health insurance, legal services and so much more) and teach you the words and terms of the industry. You'll get job tips and advice, the benefit of my experiences on the set and contact information that will help you get started and help you succeed.

So live your dream, learn how to be a good background actor/extra – and have fun doing it!

Email me with your comments and experiences at *info@jkelly4extras.com*.

Break a leg, and I'll see you in Hollywood.

— *Jo Kelly* … ON LOCATION.

About Jo

Jo Kelly is a native of the Los Angeles/Hollywood, California area who has first-hand knowledge of the film and television industry. Jo's talents are many and her enthusiasm for learning, exploring and excelling is endless. During her 25-year marriage to Jack Kelly, star of many films and the long-running, popular TV series, "Maverick," she also raised a family and ran a real estate office.

After Jack's death in the early 1990s, Jo's sister, Judi, handed her a flyer that displayed the headline, "Be a Movie Extra." Encouraged and hoping to make a career change, Jo answered the ad. She paid $135 for annual dues and got only one background acting job. She had been scammed.

On a positive note, Jo learned some BIG do's and don'ts, remained hopeful and kept trying to become a good background actor and a member of SAG. Once she learned the ropes, including the right place to register for extras work, she was on her way. In fact, the day after registering, she went to work on the set of "Providence."

Today, with her signature effervescence, Jo presents common sense techniques and unique inside secrets to breaking into the acting world through background acting seminars and in this book, *The Truth about Being an Extra (2005).*

1
Action!
Getting Started...

Getting started as a background actor (movie extra) takes a courageous step. You'll leave your comfort zone and everything that's familiar to you and venture into the world of imagination, where things are not as they may seem (or perhaps they are!), and where acting the part of a fictitious character must be carefully performed as an employee with acting goals. Come along as we take the first steps together.

Action (Background)!

You are about to embark on a fun journey. On the road to becoming a background actor ("extra"), you can participate as much or as little as you like. It's all up to you. How much or how little you invest of yourself will dictate the level of your success.

In many respects, you'll be your own boss. You'll accept the times, dates and places (or not accept them) for working. Once you've accepted, however, and once you are on the set, you must pay attention to detail, listen to directions and be punctual and professional at all times.

You may not always understand the directions you are given, and you might believe that no one will notice if you don't follow them completely. But believe me, someone will notice, and you may be asked to leave or, worse, you may get stuck on a freezing set, in "holding," away from where all the action is taking place.

Jo's Take:

Once I was told to wear flat shoes with my suit on the set. I thought how ridiculous it would look – to wear flat rubber-soled shoes with a dressy suit. It wouldn't look nice and I would never wear flats with a suit, and I want to look all "put together." It also occurred to me that my feet were not going to be filmed, so I ignored the directions given me and I wore my beautiful high heeled shoes that matched my suit. Nobody noticed and I was home free. I knew better, and I looked better, too, or so I thought. The moment arrived for my crossing* and there I was strutting my stuff in the background, while the actors said their lines – over the "click, clop, click, clop, click, clop" of my high-heeled shoes that matched my suit. The director yelled, "CUT!!!" I knew I was in trouble.

I was pulled into holding, where they keep all the extras until it's time for their scenes, and was told to sit it out. It was a bad move on my part and a BIG MISTAKE that almost cost me the job. Later, I promised to wear socks and quiet shoes and was put back on the set. I was lucky they didn't send me home.

I've made some mistakes and learned through trial and error what to do and what NOT to do. Learn from my experiences, and you'll never be booted from the set.

The World of "Extras" & Background Actors

What is an Extra?

"Extra work" refers to employment as a background actor in scenes for television or film. People who do this type of work – "extras," "atmosphere" or "background" – have no speaking lines. They are used to create realistic depictions in public places. Scenes in restaurants, courtrooms, hallways and in public usually need to be filled with people who are walking, sitting, eating or miming in the background.

What or Who is an Extra?

There are not many requirements for becoming a background actor or extra. Agencies that cast for extras look for all types. That includes people who are tall, short, fat, skinny, young, old, male, female and from all ethnic and cultural backgrounds.

Who Arranges for Extras to Get Work?

The needs for a particular scene will dictate precisely what type of extras will be cast. In Los

Angeles, there are many "extra" casting agencies, but only a few handle the bulk of the work. Some are large and some are small. The key to dealing with agencies that cast for extras is knowing whether or not they are reputable (See Chapter 2).

Networking Can Lead to Better Jobs

Extra work can be especially useful to an actor just starting out. You'll have the opportunity to see how a real television or move set operates which can help you in future acting jobs. Working as an extra is one of the ways a non-union person can become eligible to join the Screen Actors Guild (SAG).

While working as an extra, you can network and trade information with other extras about agents, casting directors and other show business related matters. Also, working as an extra on shows like soap operas can lead to "under-fives," which are speaking parts with five lines or less. Under-fives pay more than regular extra work and obviously provide more exposure than ordinary extra work.

Jo's Take

As an extra, familiarity with the way things are done, and the way you are expected to do your job, can make the difference between a short stint as a background actor and pleasing the powers that be to the point that they call you back. Know the ropes and network and you'll do well.

Notes

2
Casting Agencies

Where do you start your background acting career? At a reputable casting agency. As you'll read in my "Good, Bad and Ugly" chapter, I want you to be fully aware of the "good guys" – the established, professional casting agencies that will treat you with respect. Let's take a look at some of the best.

Getting Cast

You will get most of your work from casting agencies who cast thousands of extras every day for the background of films, commercials and movies being produced in Southern California.

The agencies listed later in this chapter are reputable, legitimate companies. I know they are, because I've worked for all of them. There are hundreds of other agencies out there, but I want to refer you to those I know you'll get work from, the ones I personally know of to be reputable, working agencies. If you're interested in registering a child, be sure to read Casting Children.

Casting Agency Basics

All agencies want you to arrive "camera ready." That means, have your hair and make-up done and look good. (Refer to my "On Set Pointers" in this book for more good advice.)

Arrive early, so you can review handouts/flyers and get the lay of the land.

Be prepared to pay the agency with cash, not credit card or check.

Take a photo identification (driver's license, passport). Although you should also take your most recent headshot photo, if you have one, you will be photographed at the agency and they will keep your photo in their database.

Casting Agency Checklist

- Photo ID
- Social Security Card (not a replica) or birth certificate
- Cash
- Pen
- Hair and make-up done (camera ready)
- Clean, neat clothing (no white clothing)
- Call the registration phone numbers in the following list, but be aware that some agencies may have changed their information since this book was researched and went to press.

■■■■■■■■

Central Casting ... ☆

220 South Flower Street
Burbank, CA 91502
818 562 2755
www.ep-services.com

Registration: Days: Monday, Wednesday and Friday; 10:30 to 11:30 a.m. (Arrive early; there are a lot of people registering with this popular agency.)

Background. I'm providing a bit more detail and history about Central Casting because it has been around since the 1920s and is the largest agency. It's the one you'll likely get most of your work from.

You should register with Central Casting before any other agency. Pre-register at the website to announce your arrival and expedite the process once you arrive in person. You'll be ahead of the game.

At Central, pick up all the handouts. They will guide you through the steps and give you the hotline numbers for getting yourself booked.

You'll have access to the hotline numbers 24/7. When you hear a message on a hotline about a job that interests you, if you fit the description of what the agency is looking for, you'll be given a "work line" number to call. Call that number for further instructions.

Once you call the workline/hotline, follow the prompts for the appropriate "team." Someone will come on the line and request your Social Security number (your "social"). They'll look you up in the computer and, if you fit the description of what they need, you'll get information including location, call time and wardrobe.

Central Casting also has "visiting days" where you are welcome to return to the agency in person to say hello and do some relationship-building with casting agents. They will see that you are serious by the fact that you are investing your time in the process. It makes a difference. If they like you, they'll call you more often. Many times, I have simply walked in to say "Hello" and been booked for a job the next morning!

▮▮▮▮▮▮▮

Sande Alessi Casting ... ☆

Aka Casting Couch
13731 Ventura Boulevard
Sherman Oaks, CA 91423
818 623-7040
www.sandealessicasting.com

Registration:

Monday – Friday, 11 a.m. to 3 p.m.
Request to register for the agency's "commercial" book. Commercial work pays more but is harder to get into.

Background Players ... ☆

6671 Sunset Boulevard
Los Angeles, CA 90028
323 790-0135

Registration:

Tuesday and Thursday, 11 a.m. to 3 p.m.
Take extra cash ($25) if you want three additional photos taken in different outfits.

Background San Diego ... ☆

4705 Ruffin Road
San Diego, CA 92123
858 974-8970
www.backgroundsandiego.com

Registration:

Pre-register online and get current dates and times. There is no registration fee and they will take photos at no cost.

Corday Productions ... ☆

"Days of Our Lives" television soap opera
3400 West Olive Avenue, Suite 315
Burbank, CA 91505
818 295-2832

Registration:

By appointment only.
No drop-offs of pictures allowed.
Call for appointment.

Bill Dance Casting ... ☆

4605 Lankershim Boulevard, Suite 401
North Hollywood, CA 91602
818 725-4208
www.billdancecasting.com

Registration:

Monday – Friday, 12 noon (you'll be there around
one hour). Check with the agency about bookings
for TV commercials

Debe Waisman Casting ... ☆

1168 Ventura Boulevard, PMB 415
Studio City, CA 91604
310 535-1325

Registration:

Free. You can mail a photo and your statistical
information to the above address or submit all
information by email to castingpics@yahoo.com

Jeff Olan Casting ... ☆

14044 Ventura Boulevard, Suite 209
Sherman Oaks, CA 91423
818 377-4475
www.jeffolancasting.com

Registration:
Daily, 11 a.m. to 2 p.m.
Take two forms of identification.

On Location Casting ... ☆

1223 Wilshire Boulevard
Santa Monica, CA 90403
310 229-5332

Registration:
Call for current registration dates.

Prime Casting ... ☆

6430 Sunset Boulevard, Suite 425
Hollywood, CA 90028
323 962-0377
www.primecasting.com

Registration:
Monday – Friday, 11 a.m. to 4 p.m.
This agency casts only commercials, so this is an excellent agency to register with for those hard-to-get commercial jobs.

Rich King Casting ... ☆

6671 Sunset Boulevard
Los Angeles, CA 90028
323 993-0100, x.301

Registration:

If you don't have photos, they will take one.
One-time only $15 cash fee.

Smith & Webster-Davis ... ☆

4924 Balboa Boulevard, Suite 431
Encino, CA 91316
310 364-3521

Registration:

Free
Mail a 3x5 photo and your pertinent information
to the above address and you will be registered.

Tina Real Casting

3108 Fifth Avenue, Suite C
San Diego, CA 92103
619 298-0544

Registration:

Tina does not have regular registration. Call for
current information.

Jo's Take

Regardless of which agency you start with,
be sure to take the "essentials" with you. ID and a
little pocket money can go a long way toward
getting your foot in the door; but knowing all the
things the agency requires is even better.

3
Casting Children

Children are special people whose acting careers require careful attention. In this chapter, I've included listings of agencies that I feel treat kids properly, agencies you can trust.

Casting Children

There are a lot of scams and unethical agencies that prey upon parents who see their children as talented, gorgeous kids "perfect" for television and film. It's important for parents to work with known agencies that are solidly established in the business and enjoy reputations for excellence and professionalism.

Parents should understand the child labor laws and the legal responsibilities for themselves and the agencies when signing contracts for their children. You can find the link for the child labor laws at www.dir.ca.gov/dlse/DLSE-CL.htm.

Obtain an application for an Entertainment Work Permit from any division of the Labor Standards Enforcement office in California or online at www.dir.ca.gov. The district office is located at:

Division of Labor Standards Enforcement
320 West Fourth Street, Suite 450
Los Angeles, CA 90013
213 620-6330

Please note that you must show your child's original Social Security card to the agency, along with a current work permit. These are required when registering a Minor (any person under the age of eighteen).

Here for your consideration are some of the reputable agencies for casting children as extras and background actors.

▪▪▪▪▪▪▪▪

Sande Alessi Casting ... ☆

Aka Casting Couch
13731 Ventura Boulevard
Sherman Oaks, CA 91423
818 623-7040
www.sandealessicasting.com

Registration:
Monday – Friday, 11 a.m. to 3 p.m.
Request to register for the agency's "commercial" book. Commercial work pays more but is harder to get into.

Background San Diego ... ☆

4705 Ruffin Road
San Diego, CA 92123
858 974-8970
www.backgroundsandiego.com

Registration:
Pre-register online and get current dates and times. There is no registration fee and they will take photos at no cost.

Christophere Gray Casting ... ☆

8271 Melrose Avenue
Los Angeles, CA 90048
323 658-1530
www.christopheregraycasting.com

Registration:
By appointment only

Hollywood Talent Association ... ☆

7825 Fay Avenue, Suite 200
La Jolla, CA 92037
858 456-5770

Registration:
Call for current information

Kids Background Talent ... ☆

207 S. Flower Street, Second Floor
Burbank, CA 91502
818 239-1371
www.kidsmanagement.com

Registration:
$25 registration fee; $30 photo fee. Bi-annual
dues are $18 to $27 (Kids under age five pay $18
every six months; kids over age five pay $27
every six months.)

Kids Hollywood Connection ... ☆

1151 Dove Street, Suite 225
Newport Beach, CA 92660
949 851-0920
www.kidshollywood.com

Registration:
Monday through Friday, by appointment only.
There is a $125 consultation fee to determine
what the child is right for, e.g., background, print,
principal work, etc.

On Location Casting ... ☆

1223 Wilshire Boulevard
Santa Monica, CA 90403
310 229-5332

Registration:
Call for current registration information.

Prime Casting ... ☆

6430 Sunset Boulevard, Suite 425
Hollywood, CA 90028
323 962-0377
www.primecasting.com

Registration:
Monday – Friday, 11 a.m. to 4 p.m.
They only cast commercials, so this is a good
place to register for those hard-to-get commercial
assignments. SAG members get a discounted fee.

Screen Children's Casting ... ☆

4000 Riverside Drive, Suite A
Burbank, CA 91505
818 846-4300

Registration:
Send a non-returnable photo with a self-addressed
stamped envelope. Write the following informa-

tion on the back side of the photo: Child's name, birthday, phone number and address. If interested, they will contact you with further information. There is a $40 fee for registration, photo and orientation and a 15 percent commission per paycheck. They primarily book newborns, however, their age range is fifteen days and up. Note: Screen Children's Casting has been casting children since 1936.

Studio Kids Management ... ⭐

15068 Rosecrans Avenue
La Mirada, CA 90638
562 902-9838, ext. 2 and the # sign
Email: studiokidscasting@aol.com

Registration:

Call or email for current information.
Registration fee $50, photo fee $50; 15 percent commission per paycheck.

They look for twins, triplets and quadruplets. Send a picture of your child/children with a self-addressed stamped envelope and they will provide a complete casting packet for you to complete and take with you to registration.

Of course, there are many more agencies that cast children as background actors. Check with your local chamber of commerce for casting agency members and with the Better Business Bureau to learn their track record.

From One Mother to Another

Sometimes a child embraces her dreams so passionately that everything else in her life becomes secondary. The unrealistic image to which she devotes herself dictates her activities – and her diet. The child with anorexic tendencies has a picture in her mind of what she ought to look like, and it doesn't look like she looks at the moment. The picture and the goal are distorted and lead her down a self destructing path. I'd like to share with you the experience of my friend, Melody, and her daughter, Jackie, to help you work toward a healthy balance as you support your child in his or her effort to build an acting or performing career.

Jackie became obsessed with exercise and food and eventually became anorexic. She was a popular girl at school, where she was a straight A student. She sang and danced professionally, was the International Pocket Nutrition Teen Spokesperson, performed on national television and in film and, with her mother, spoke to groups about self esteem.

Her mother, Melody, recalls that, "on camera and at school, she was totally confident. At school she was a leader with her friends." Jackie swam 50 to 100 laps a day and worked out two hours a day, to stay slim. She limited her diet to particular foods (mostly yogurt) and insisted her mother purchase certain foods from specialty stores.

Melody worked with her daughter, providing loving care, support and guidance. The following may be signs to watch for if your child is under pressure to be "the best," including the need to achieve lofty goals or impress others with her skill or beauty. Melody observed many of these characteristics in Jackie, who is now a healthy, happy and productive young lady:

Constantly feeling cold (from lack of nourishment), noticeable weight loss, constant food analysis and weighing, claiming not to be hungry, feeling depressed or anxious, isolating herself, wearing loose-fitting clothes to hide weight loss, denial of a problem, developing fine, downy hair on arms, dry and brittle fingernails and hair, yellowish skin tone, inability to receive compliments, denying her beauty; negativity, ceasing of menstrual periods, quitting activities she once loved, moodiness, sensitivity; and other unusual behavior.

What can you do to help your child get well? Professional help should be a priority, starting with a carefully chosen doctor and counselor. Complement professional assistance by helping your child see her relationship with reality. Nudge her lovingly but firmly back to health. Ask questions to learn what may be troubling her, listening closely to what she says and observing her body language and verbal expression. Help her develop her faith. Improve communication with her and spend more one-on-one time discussing things of importance to her. Set goals. Resolve your own conflicts so you are yourself well adjusted. Associate with healthy people, teach healthy food choices, exhibit a winning attitude and encourage her to develop her talents.

As your child becomes more enthralled with her future as an actor, stay in touch. Don't add unnecessary (or unrealistic) pressure for achievement or appearance. Ask lots of questions, keep the lines of communication open, and stay healthy and happy together.

Jo's Take

I included the above story because I think it's really important for us to have our sensitivity antennae up when we're around the children in our lives. It's so easy for a child to disappear into the background of his or her room, to camouflage the problems. Love them and care for them; they are such precious people.

4
Calling Services

The goal of a Calling Service is to get background acting jobs for you. But you need to know which calling services will really work consciously on your behalf. So let's take a look at ways to learn more about the calling services you might consider.

Calling Services

"Calling services" are companies you hire to book you for work. Let's say you're tired of calling all the hotlines and listening to long recorded messages only to learn there's no opening that describes you. You might just want to hire a calling service.

Here's how it works.

You visit the websites and learn as much as you can about the calling services, and then you make a selection. You then visit the calling service in person to register, have your picture taken, and pay the first and last months' fees.

Fees vary according to the company. Some calling services give a price break to people over the age of 50. Some are selective about taking SAG background actors, however, they always want non-union new clients.

With a calling service contract, you'll work three or four days a week, perhaps more. You can advise the calling service of any restrictions you might have, about where and when you are willing to work. For example, as a resident of Mission Viejo in South Orange County, you may not wish to drive to Valencia, north of Los Angeles, where shooting of the popular "JAG" series took place. They will honor your restrictions.

Also, if you don't want to work an all-nighter (when you start work around 4 p.m. and get wrapped around 6 or 7 a.m.), let them know. Once your restrictions are entered into the database, they are honored.

Although there are many calling services, when you sign with Central Casting, they will inform you about Extras Management, which is across the street from Central. As a SAG actor, I used Extras Management for several years and was very happy with them. As you work and network with fellow actors, you'll hear about other calling services and you can make up your own mind when and if you decide to hire one.

My advice is to try to book yourself for a while with casting agencies, registering with as many reputable agencies as possible. Then, after gaining some experience and learning the ropes, you may decide to hire a calling service. Just check with as many background actors as possible to learn about their experiences with various calling services.

Once you settle on two or three calling services, visit their websites to learn their requirements. (Remember never to wear white when you go to register and have your picture taken.)

███████

Atmosphere Talent ... ☆

6671 Sunset Boulevard, Suite 1525-1
Hollywood, CA 90028
323 469-7700
www.atmospheretalent.com

Registration:
$50 to register and $50 monthly.

Background Talent Services ... ☆

4804 Laurel Canyon Boulevard, Suite 414
North Hollywood, CA 91607
Main Line: 818 760-7090
Registration Line: 818 771-5727

Registration:
They book mostly non-union extras for commercials and music videos and pay from $100 to $160 per day. This would be a good calling service for non-union, because commercials and music videos always pay more than regular background work.

Cameo Casting Services ... ☆

6115 Selma Avenue, #203
Hollywood, CA 90028
Registration Line: 323 460-4475
www.cameocasting.com
Email: extras@yocameo.com

Registration:
$29 and $65/month. First and last are due unless you use a credit card or debit card, in which case

they will waive the last month. You must call first and set an appointment. Be willing to work all of Los Angeles and surrounding areas.

Extras Management ... ☆
207 S. Flower Street, Second Floor
Burbank, CA 91502
Main Line: 818 972-9474
Registration Line: 818 771-8466
www.extrasmanagement.com

Registration:
$70/month, first and last plus $10 photo fee. Registration time is 10 a.m. to 2 p.m. Extras Management has strong ties with Central Casting, which might make it more desirable for getting booked. I was with this calling service until I began work on this book and found they did a good job for me.

Jo's Take

Good luck as you explore the calling services, remember: It's a job, a wonderful opportunity – and you can have fun doing it.

Notes

5
Talent Agencies

How does a Talent Agency differ from a Calling Service or a Casting Agency? Let me count the ways.

Talent Agencies: Just the Facts

Experienced actors moving into the mainstream of television and film may be interested to know about talent agencies. You'll be ready for an agent, a business manager or a talent agency once you've landed some more substantial roles (beyond the "extras" experience). Perhaps some of these questions and answers will help acquaint you with the types of agencies:

Q: What is the difference between a legitimate talent agency and one whose purpose is to separate you from your money?

A: The legitimate talent agency does not charge a fee payable in advance for registration, for resumes, public relations services, screen tests, photographs or acting lessons. If you are signed as a client by a reputable talent agency, you will pay nothing until you work. A commission of 10 to 15 percent of your earnings must be agreed upon in advance.

Most legitimate talent agencies do not advertise for clients in newspapers nor do they solicit through the mail, the Internet or by approaching you at shopping malls.

Q: Are reputable talent agencies licensed by the State of California?

A: Yes. Such talent agencies are licensed by the State as Artists' Managers and most established agencies in the motion picture and television industries are also franchised by the Screen Actors Guild. You should be extremely careful of any talent agency not licensed in your state.

Q: What about personal managers and business managers?

A: There are well established firms in the business of personal management and business management. Such firms, however, typically handle established artists and do not advertise for new clients.

Remember, this information is for the individual who has decided to pursue an acting career beyond that of a background actor.

Jo's Take

I can't answer all your questions in this book, so feel free to contact me through my web site at **www.jkelly4extras.com** or send me a note through email: **info@jkelly4extras.com.**

Notes

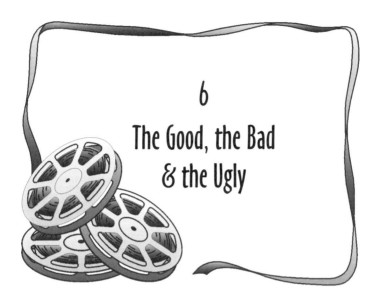

6
The Good, the Bad
& the Ugly

You knew this chapter would be included in my book somewhere, right? Here's a heads-up on scams and pitfalls, along with customary fees. So here you go ... pay close attention and you'll enjoy smooth sailing into your background acting career.

The Good, The Bad & The Ugly

Things to Watch Out For

For those who want to go beyond background acting, who aspire to celebrity status or want to perform in speaking roles at a higher level in the acting profession, I'd like to alert you to a few situations you may encounter in your career. Be prepared for:

Bait and Switch. A good example of a bait-and-switch situation is the person who answers an ad for "Talented People" or "Model Search" and learns that the "agency" can only use you IF you purchase their pictures or enroll in their classes. The ad is only bait. Many people grab it and end up spending their hard-earned dollars for products that never land them a satisfactory job. There are numerous companies claiming to cast extras that charge exorbitant fees, list false credits and rarely or never call you for work. They often advertise in large circulation newspapers and sometimes post flyers on utility poles. Beware of the promises from companies that don't deliver.

Employment Fees & Unreasonable Fees. California State Labor Code prohibits employers or potential employers from demanding payment for employment opportunities. If you reside and work outside California, check with your state labor board for the current law there.

The industry standard registration fee for legitimate background casting agencies is approximately $25. This fee covers the cost of taking your photo.

No SAG Approval for Agents or Agencies. If you're shopping for an agent, make sure they are approved by the Screen Actors Guild. You should only audition for major film or commercial roles through a SAG-approved agent. By the way, SAG rules prevent its agents from operating classes and selling photography services. And someone who offers to sell you a SAG voucher is not legitimate. To check on SAG approval of an agency in Hollywood, call 213 954-1600.

Photography Services and Packages that Cost More Than $400. You don't really need a headshot (or an extensive resume) to get background work. All you need are your physical measurements (height, weight, hips, waist) and a 3x5 color photo of yourself against a white background. It does not have to be professional, although a professional photo makes a good impression. It must represent how you look now, today. Most extra agencies will take a photo of you, usually digital or Polaroid, for a minimal fee (which really should not be more than $20-$25).

Magazines Making Promises. Articles and advertisements that promise to publish your picture to all the important people and decision makers in the entertainment industry.

Internet Come-ons. Promises to publish your picture to all the important people and decision makers in the entertainment industry.

No State Approval for Classes. People teaching classes in California are required to be approved or certified by the State of California. Many acting schools entice newcomers with the dream of learning the craft of acting by enrolling in acting classes. Not only are the schools not approved, but there are no likely job prospects. Want to check on a school's certification? Call 916 445-3427.

Bargain Prices at Acting Schools. Any school of good repute has overhead to meet and won't offer rock bottom prices. Make sure you know exactly what you are getting when you compare prices. How many classes are offered? Is a student or a professional acting coach teaching the class? How many "Agent Nights" are included in the price? May parents attend? How many guest speakers will participate? Typically, a school that charges really low prices makes their money by selling photography packages and other products, or they are not offering quality. The adage, *You get what you pay for,* is appropriate.

Jo's Take

There are certainly legitimate classes offered by casting directors and producers. These are typically ongoing, "traditional" acting classes.

Notes

7
The
First Day

Is it your first day on the set? Are butterflies dancing around inside you yet? Do you have a list of don't forget's? Here's my helping hand. I've forgotten enough essential accessories and ended up in enough predicaments to write a chapter just about the first day do's and don'ts. You'll find most of these pointers will be true of almost any day on a background acting assignment.

The First Day

Prepare and Be Prepared!

Know Where You are Going. You will be provided with directions to the set or location, but plan the night before and take the time to get acquainted with the area. Using Mapquest.com is a good idea, but you should also invest in your own copy of the Thomas Bros. Guide for Los Angeles and Orange counties. This is an easy-to-use book of maps with detailed views of neighborhoods and larger views of the freeway systems and exits. (Keep this great reference in your car.)

If you ride the bus, know the routes, plan ahead and, if you need more information, call or look up the website for the transit authority in your area. You can access transit information online at www.transitweb.its.dot.gov.

Be Punctual. Always arrive fifteen minutes before your scheduled call time. If you are late, the casting company that booked you WILL be notified and this could affect your being called again or sent home for the day.

Only Park in a Designated Area. Parking for "Extras" will be clearly marked.

Sign In Immediately. When you are booked by the casting agency, you will be given the name of your contact person. Your contact will probably be the Assistant Director (AD) or the Second Assistant Director.

When you arrive, find your contact person before doing anything else. The first reason is so they will know you arrived early. The second reason is to get your voucher so your total number of hours worked is accurate. (This makes a difference if your work schedule extends into overtime.)

Be Available the ENTIRE Day of the Shoot. That means ALL day and ALL night. Don't make plans for "after the shoot." When you agree to work, you are expected to honor your commitment and stay until you are wrapped.

You might be on the set for ten, twelve or fourteen hours or more. California state law states the minimum wage is $6.75/hour or $54/8 for extra performers. If you are employed for more than eight hours, you are to receive time-and-one-half pay for the ninth and tenth hours worked and double time for all hours worked after the tenth hour until the sixteenth hour. In the background acting business, the sixteenth hour is called Golden Time. On Golden Time, you receive $54 per hour for every hour worked over the sixteenth hour.

It is impossible to foresee how many hours you will work, as that is contingent upon many other variables, including the schedules of the lead actors, the number of takes*, weather, lighting and other unpredictable challenges on the set.

DO NOT Hang Around After Being Wrapped. That is a no-no. They need you to leave as soon as you are wrapped.

Get Your Voucher Signed Before You Leave. Your signed voucher is the only way to ensure that you'll be paid for the time you spend on the set. Always keep your voucher until you get your paycheck.

Jo's Take

I worked on a Coca Cola commercial in a mansion in Malibu and we had worked fourteen hours. At the end of the day, my friend, Suzanne, and I put our heads together and decided to get a head start on the mass exit of extras from the set. We jumped in the van before everyone else, to be driven back to base camp to get signed out.

Upon our arrival at base camp, we learned the AD was still at the mansion – signing everyone out. My feet were killing me, and I didn't want to walk back up the hill and wait in line. I said to Suzanne, "Let's go. They'll mail us our checks." Suzanne, a 20-year veteran, insisted we go back to the mansion to get our vouchers signed, explaining that the only proof we would have that we had worked was to get our vouchers signed. I was still willing to risk it, but Suzanne wouldn't hear of it.

As you probably guessed, Suzanne was right. It was the holiday season and, for whatever reason, it took six weeks (not the norm) to get paid. Had we not gotten our vouchers signed, we would not have had any proof that we had worked.

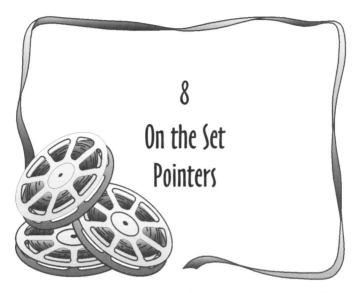

8
On the Set Pointers

Should you bring a friend? Will you be standing around twiddling your thumbs a lot? How can you be comfortable when you're standing in high-heeled shoes? There are a myriad of situations that can directly affect your comfort level, your ability to complete your assignment professionally and the likelihood you will be called back. I've tried to cover the basics here.

On the Set Pointers

Inside Tips that Make a Difference

No Visitors Allowed. Friends are not allowed to meet you on the set or in the holding area. If you're trying to help someone become an extra, inviting them on the set is not the right way to go.

Always Arrive "Camera Ready," with Extra Clothes. Arrive dressed properly with your hair and make-up done. Bring three complete wardrobe changes or optional sets of clothing in a wardrobe bag. But don't overpack. No logos or obvious brand names are allowed, so forget about the shirt with the message or the high class icon. Your clothes must be clean and pressed. It is very important to not make any changes once you have been checked and approved by Hair, Make-up and Wardrobe. Believe me, they are watching everybody.

Quiet on the Set! It's important to be quiet on the set. Turn off your cell phone and pager and your personal digital assistant and keep your voice down or don't talk at all.

Bring Some "Busy Work." Bring a book, magazine, dictionary or *The History of The World* (Parts I and II), since you may find yourself in Holding for a while. Do not bring anything that makes noise – not even a radio with headset, since it might keep you from hearing your call to the set. You may be in Holding for a while, but it is also a GREAT time to network and get to know your fellow background actors. I have made many good friends and learned a lot about this industry in Holding.

Jo's Comfort & Safety Pointers

Here's a little FYI from me to you in no particular order. These are just a few of my personal tips. They are not requirements, but they'll help make your life as a background actor a whole lot easier.

Network, Network, Network.

Be courteous to everyone and get to know "who's who" on the set. Your regular background actors know the ropes and can teach you a lot. There are many people who make their living as background actors and many who start in acting and may become celebrities in years to come. You could be enjoying lunch with the Director's son or daughter. Mind your Ps and Qs.

Fill Your Gas Tank the Night Before.

There is no accounting for getting lost and I have gotten L-O-S-T many times! Aside from that, you may be called at 9 p.m. for a 6 a.m. call. That means you'll rise VERY early and the last thing

In life, as in film, w

all background actors

you want to do at 4:30 in the morning, when you are trying to allow ample driving time to adjust for traffic jams in Los Angeles traffic, is try to find an open gas station. Be prepared.

Keep a Pen with You and in Your Car.

You'll need a pen to complete paperwork. Just like when you go for a job interview, if you don't have a pen, you'll appear to be unprepared and disorganized. Besides, no one likes to share their own pen in the office or on the set. This is especially true of the AD, who needs that pen and doesn't have time to wait for you.

Get Connected.

Invest in a cell phone, pager, voice mail or answering machine. When casting agents call to book you and can't find you, someone else gets the job.

Avoid Carpooling.

You could get released for the day, but your friend in a different scene has to stay, and stay, and stay. You're left tired and bored, waiting for your carpool partner.

Take a Seat (With You).

Buy an inexpensive folding chair or chair in a bag. It will come in handy for long shoots on location, help you grab a bit of rest and keep you refreshed.

Ladies, Bring Flats.

If you're wearing heels (as in high-heeled shoes) and it's a long day, flat-heeled shoes will give your feet a much deserved break while you're in the Holding area.

Jo's Take

(How a Little Gossip Got Us in a Big To-Do)

On a commercial I worked as a non-union extra at the Los Angeles Tennis Club, we background actors worked with SAG extras and I happened to meet up with a very nice SAG gal, who I'll call Joan, who I had worked with on a previous assignment. She said Hi and asked if I was with Lisa (not her real name), another "extra" friend. I replied, "Yes, she's in the bleachers. Joan said to say 'Hello' to Lisa for her."

As a SAG background actor, Joan had better accommodations than those of us who worked as non-union extras. I told Lisa that Joan had expressed her regards and Lisa made disparaging remarks, both to me and to others. Finally, a man standing next to Lisa remarked, "That SAG gal is my wife."

Lisa, as would be expected, came to me very upset and said, "I just put my foot in my mouth," and she told me what had happened.

Later, she tried to apologize to Joan's husband and ask him to not tell her about the remarks. We both knew, however, that he would relay the story to Joan and to our Assistant Director.

The result was that neither Lisa nor I ever worked for that Assistant Director again. You see, I was guilty by association.

It's so important to behave professionally. When you park your car, park all your suspicions, jealousies and petty complaints as well. Choose friends who act in a mature, adult and professional manner.

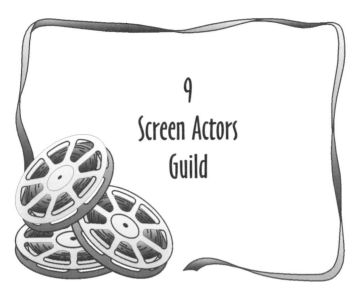

9
Screen Actors Guild

Should you join the Screen Actors Guild (SAG)? How will you become eligible? And how will membership benefit you? This chapter shares some of the high points and requirements of this prestigious union for performers and background actors.

Working with the Screen Actors Guild (SAG)

The Screen Actors Guild was established in 1933 and has a long history of working to enhance actors' working conditions, benefits and compensation. (Learn more at www.sag.org).

Once you have fulfilled the requirements to join SAG, you'll find there are many perks that come with membership. Among them are vision, dental and health insurance benefits. Another little perk is the Screen Actors Guild magazine, a quarterly publication that keeps you up-to-date on all activities, negotiations, labor laws and background acting information.

SAG on the move

The SAG background actors system is changing as I write, but I'll share with you the most recent information available. The current system requires you to have three SAG vouchers to be eligible for SAG membership.

In 2005, a transition team of background community members created a new eligibility system based on points rather than vouchers. The national board approved the plan, but it was forced into a holding state until funding was approved and a group of background actors selected to test the new plan. SAG will probably be well into 2006 before the system is properly in place.

New SAG eligibility rules

In the new plan, the transition team's goals in requiring points (vs. vouchers) from background actors were to cut down on corruption that had infiltrated the voucher system and to increase the professionalism of new background members. Under the new rules, background actors must put in their time on sets before they gain SAG membership.

Points are earned by working on a job with a signatory production company within one of the background zones and by attending seminars on various aspects of the business of acting. The employment must be in a SAG film, videotape, television program or commercial and proof of having worked the job is required. All SAG productions require that a percentage of the work go to non-union extras. The seminars are being developed in conjunction with SAG's Member Education department. The new twist to the points system is that non-members can get points by working non-union background positions on SAG projects. This does not mean that once actors are in the Guild they can work non-union jobs. It only means that while they are seeking eligibility, they get rewarded for hard work and learning the craft of acting. Once they are SAG union members, they work only union covered jobs. If you are interested in SAG membership and have met the eligibility requirements, contact your nearest SAG office before actually visiting the SAG office, to arrange for an appointment.

As a SAG member, you'll have dues, however, you will be paid double wages and have health benefits and you'll be represented by your union if a dispute arises, a big Plus. For more details, visit www.sag.org.

Jo's Take

It would be great if all of us could make lots of money doing background acting. Unfortunately, the nature of the job dictates otherwise. That's why I heartily advise working toward your eligibility to join SAG.

10
Wardrobe

What you wear and how you look speaks volumes about who you are, your self image, how you want to be seen and what you're after in life. By the same token, how well prepared you are for your assignment, from a wardrobe point of view, is highly important. Take a look ...

Wardrobe

Let's talk about how you're going to dress for your agency assignment. Proper outfitting can really make you look good. On the other hand, because you are judged so clearly by your appear-

ance and preparedness in the acting business, getting a less than passing "score" in this department can negatively affect your career progress.

When you receive your instructions from the hotline phone regarding your time, location and wardrobe, you'll know how they want you to dress. They will usually instruct you to "wear one and bring two."

Wardrobe people wield enough power to make your life uncomfortable, so let's not upset them. Wear an outfit that fits the description given on the recorded message; and bring two other similar outfits.

If the wardrobe people do not like anything you are wearing or have brought with you, they can put you into studio clothes. Try your best to avoid letting that happen, because if they decide to change your wardrobe, you have to give them your voucher, which you will not get back until you are wrapped (finished for the day).

At the end of a long day, having been outfitted in studio clothes by Wardrobe, you are required to go and change back into your own clothes. Then you stand in line to return the studio clothes and get your voucher back. Then you get to stand in another line to get your voucher signed by the AD. If you're working a large call, this process could take more time than you really want it to, possibly making a 12 hour work day much longer. And that's no fun.

Here's what I found works well for me. I give Wardrobe what I call a "throw away:"

Wear two gold chains instead of one, a sweater around your shoulders, a scarf that is really not necessary, etc. They usually say to me: You're fine, but lose one chain; or, lose the scarf, etc. It has worked for me. You'll figure out what works best for you and set your own routine.

Remember, it is important to pay attention to the recorded instructions. People who pay attention are always remembered. Pictures will be taken of everyone on the set and you could be asked back if they see professionalism in you. Being a good background actor by giving them what they want will pay off.

Looking for an inexpensive way to shop for clothes?

Try consignment and thrift shops for those items you may not have in your closet, for scarves, gloves, funky jewelry, uniforms (e.g., nurses and military uniforms), 1950s and 1960s style clothes and shoes. Production loves it when you already appear wearing clothing of the era in which you will be acting. Wigs are important for the ladies. In fact, having your photo taken wearing different wigs will get you more work.

Jo's Take

Wardrobe is one of those areas where you just must pay attention to instructions given on the agency's recorded message. Take your throw aways with you but always give them what they want. That's the best way to get asked back.

11
Production Studios

Once you begin accepting assignments as a background actor, you may find it handy to keep this book, including the list of production studios in this chapter, in your car for quick reference.

Production Studios

Recently, I had the occasion to work on a pilot at the Warner Ranch in Burbank, California, which brought to mind the first time I worked a pilot at that location. You see, I went to Warner Brothers studio the first time, and that's a very different place. The second time, I did it right.

I thought it might be helpful to you if I list several of the major studios, so you won't make the mistake I made. This may come in handy when you have a call and you have listened to the long recorded message several times (wardrobe, location, call time, parking, etc.) and still did not get all the details (there's always a lot of information because of the different categories and types of actors needed for different scenes).

■■■■■■■

ABC Studios
4151 Prospect Avenue
Hollywood, CA 90027
310 557-7777

CBS Television Center
7800 Beverly Boulevard
Los Angeles, CA 90036
213 852-2345

Culver Studios

9336 W. Washington Boulevard
Culver City, CA 90232
310 836-5537

Fox Television Center/KTTV

5746 Sunset Boulevard
Hollywood, CA 90028
323 856-1000

Majestic Studios

5760 Tujunga Avenue
North Hollywood, CA 91601
818 505-1184

Metro Goldwyn Mayer (MGM)

10250 Constellation Avenue
Los Angeles, CA 90007
310 449-3000

Metro Goldwyn Mayer United Artists

2500 Broadway
Santa Monica, CA 90404
310 449-3000

NBC

3000 Alameda Avenue
Burbank, CA 91523
818 840-4444

Oceanside Studios
3350 Ocean Park Boulevard
Santa Monica, CA 90405
310 399-7704

Paramount Ranch
8800 Grimes Canyon Road
Moorpark, CA 93021
805 530-1967

Paramount Studios
5555 Melrose Avenue
Hollywood, CA 90038
323 956-5000

Production Group
1330 N. Vine Street
Hollywood, CA 90028
323 462-2300

Raleigh Studios
5300 Melrose Avenue
Hollywood, CA 90004
323 466-3111

Raleigh Studios
1600 Rosecrans Avenue
Manhattan Beach, CA 90266
323 466-3111

Sony Studios
10202 W. Washington Boulevard
Culver City, CA 90232
310 244-4000

South Bay Studios
20434 S. Santa Fe Avenue
Long Beach, CA 90810

Sunset Gower Studios
(NBC Hollywood)
1438 N. Gower Street
Hollywood, CA 90028
323 467-1001

Sunset Stage
6063 Sunset Boulevard
Hollywood, CA 90028
323 461-6308

The Lot
1041 N. Formosa
Hollywood, CA 90046
323 850-2500

Twentieth Century Fox
10201 Pico Boulevard
Culver City, CA 90067
310 369-1000

Universal Studios/MCA
100 Universal City Plaza
Universal City, CA 91608
818 777-3000

Valencia Studios
26030 Avenue Hall
Valencia, CA 91355
661 702-9102

Walt Disney Studios

500 S. Buena Vista Street
Burbank, CA 91506
818 560-1000

Warner Brothers Studios

4000 Warner Boulevard
Burbank, CA 91522
818 954-2577

Warner Hollywood Studios

1041 N. Formosa
Hollywood, CA 90046
323 850-2500

Warner Ranch

411 N. Hollywood Way
Burbank, CA 91505
818 954-2577

World TV Productions

6611 Santa Monica Boulevard
Hollywood, CA 90038
323 469-5638

Jo's Take

You will rarely have a reason to call any of
the studios I've listed here, other than for the
purpose of getting directions or cross streets.

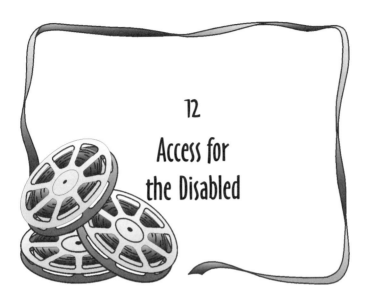

12

Access for the Disabled

More and more, studios and casting agencies are placing people with disabilities in the roles of the disabled and abled people in film, television and commercials. Read up on your rights and opportunities in the pages that follow.

Access for Performers with Disabilities

In researching the Web for more information for this book, I discovered this website which some of you might find of interest:

www.disabilityemployment.org/med_acc.htm

This site gives visitors a wonderful treasury of information about jobs for people with disabilities, including information on acting and background jobs. Its Media Access Office was established by the California Governor's Committee on Employment of People with Disabilities and entertainment and media industry professionals. It serves as a liaison for casting directors looking for actors with disabilities.

A number of individuals and organizations exist for the purpose of increasing awareness and advocating reform on behalf of people with disabilities, including people specifically working or seeking work in the entertainment industry. The push is to replace able actors who are acting the parts of disabled people with actors who actually have those disabilities or limited functions.

Further research on the disability employment site led me to a company that specializes in helping background actors obtain extra work in the film industry. The company is:

Media Access
4640 Lankershim Boulevard, Suite 305,
North Hollywood, CA 91602
Phone 818 752-1196
Registration is free.

Media Access has operated since 1980. They are an advocacy group and they serve as a casting liaison for performers with disabilities. To register, call and request a new client packet. Make an appointment to visit the agency personally, when you can submit finished paperwork and photos.

You should submit a headshot and a photo that shows your disability (if it is visible in your photo).

Media Access uses both non-union and union actors. Their office will submit headshots and resumes to casting directors and will provide special information about accessibility and special services. Their services include: individual career development, reviewing and setting career goals, industry referrals, acting workshops, low-cost headshot clinics and young performers and parent seminars.

Jo's Take
I think this is certainly worth a shot for anyone with a disability who possesses a strong desire to enter the acting field as an extra or actor. It could prove fruitful and fun.

Notes

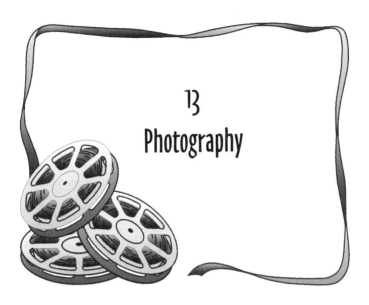

13
Photography

I could publish a list of professional photographers in this chapter, but since Rich Hogan of Rich Hogan Photography is the best of the best, I'll share him with you.

Photographers

Sooner or later, every aspiring actor must present a professional photograph of himself or herself. This is not the photo taken by your husband, your girlfriend, your parent or your best friend. It's the one you, very smartly, sought a professional photographer to take. The one that shows your best, who you really are and what you can bring to pictures.

Rich Hogan with Jay Leno.

Hollywood photographer Rich Hogan, who is the official photographer at Sunset Casting, has worked at his profession since 1990. From his famous corner at Hollywood and Vine, he has photographed celebrity clients including Magic Johnson, Tina Turner, Richard Simmons and many of the actors and entertainers you see on major television networks. One of his most famous local clients is "Big Boy," the popular talk show host heard during L.A.'s morning drive time on Power 106 FM Radio.

Rich's photographs have helped many actors and actresses get "the Call" that led to starring roles in movies and TV. As a result of one of the looks he helped to create, a client received eighteen guest appearances on Jay Leno's "Tonight" show.

In addition to actors, Rich also photographs musical groups and CD covers. His photos have appeared on magazine covers, billboards and in fashion magazines.

Rich has been featured as one of Hollywood's top photographers in numerous publications including *LA Weekly, The Los Angeles Times, Los Angeles Magazine, Variety, Academy Players Directory, Music Connection, The Hollywood Reporter* and many others.

Rich has also been featured by Judy Kerr, the dialogue coach for the "Seinfeld" TV series, in the popular "Acting is Everything."

Rich Hogan's color department enjoys a rating as "The Best" of all the photographers in town. He's also proud of the fact that of all the thousands of photographers in Los Angeles, he was selected by Time Warner to be featured in the video, "The Making of a Headshot."

Rich is featured in the yearly headshot edition of Backstage West. Even some of the members of the SAG and AFTRA Boards of Directors have used him for their headshots and these photos can be seen in many of their organizations' publications.

Local radio stations, including KPWR, KBIG, KFWB and KRLA, have all saluted Rich on the air.

I have used many photographers during my years as a model and background actor, most of them good. However, I have found that Rich will go that extra mile for you. He is honest, professional and his prices are the best in Hollywood. I've used Rich for all my professional needs for the last five years. I highly recommend Rich and know your experience with him will be good.

> Rich Hogan
> Phone: 323 467-2628
> Email: richhoganphotography@hotmail.com
> Website: richhogancreative.com

Jo's Take

Rich is the official photographer for Sunset Casting, which shoots commericals with non-union people only. Remember that commercials pay more than $100 a day, so call and sign-up.

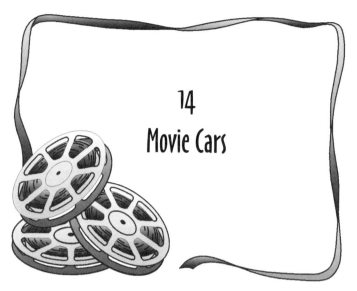

14
Movie Cars

How about getting a paycheck for your car? That's a lot better proposition than having that piece of metal just sit in a parking lot soaking up the Hollywood sun all day. Here's how...

Movie Cars

When you register with Casting Agencies, you may want to list your car. If all goes well, you will get a call to work and the call will request that you bring your car as well.

Agencies pay between $35 and $50 extra per day for the use of the car. There are a few agencies, however, that do not place people; they only place cars. Their fees and payment rates vary, so check with each one separately to learn the rules. Here are the ones I am aware of:

▪▪▪▪▪▪▪

Specialty Vehicle Association
P.O. Box 3303
Chatsworth, CA 91311
818 882-2927

Special Info: This agency specializes in cars manufactured from 1900 to 1960. Your best bet is to send photos of your car (inside and out) to "Chuck." (Send by postal mail or email them to SVAchuck@aol.com.) Tell him the condition of the car and he will contact you if he has a need for a vehicle like yours.

Hollywood Picture Cars
1028 N. La Brea Avenue
West Hollywood, CA 90038
323 466-2277 (CARS)
www.hollywoodpicturecars.com

Show Mobiles
5542 Cahuenga Boulevard
North Hollywood, CA 91601
818 762-0700
www.showmobiles.com

Picture Vehicles Unlimited
10615 Chandler Boulevard
North Hollywood, CA 91601
818 766-2200
www.picturevehicles.com

Nationwide Picture Cars
8491 Sunset Boulevard, Suite 269
Hollywood, CA 90069
310 659-1711
www.nationwidepicturecars.com

Jo's Take

Here's me and my movie car at the Riviera in Westminster, CA, where I have been privileged to present several background actor seminars.

Notes

15
The Business of Background Acting

Background acting is a job. It's one of the few jobs you get that is "work" while it's also "fun." But after work, there are bills to pay and Uncle Sam to report to. Here are a few tips to make the business side of background acting a little more manageable.

The Business of Background Acting

It goes without saying that the overall management of your background acting career is in your hands, especially if you fulfill assignments for more than one agency, or assignments on different film projects or if you are your own agent.

This means the need to maintain good records is essential. Here are some suggestions to help you set up your recordkeeping system, both for tax reporting and just staying in control and knowing where you've been and where you're headed.

Recommended Files

Agency files. In a box, filing cabinet or portable file, keep all your paystubs as well as any pertinent tax information you will need at the end of the year.

Financial files. Keep a running list or spreadsheet of your assignments with dates, rates of pay and taxes withheld by the employer or agency.

End-of-Year Activities

Page through your files and copy or retrieve any documents containing information pertinent to the year just ending. Categorize them for ease of reporting and you'll be better prepared than most (and your tax preparer will think you're the greatest).

   Expenses. Keep all receipts and documentation for expenses related to your work and background acting calls. You must provide your accountant or tax preparer with the precise amounts of money totaled for the tax deductible expenses areas (not a guess), and these totals will come directly from your receipts.

   David Rogers and Sid Wilner of Actors Tax Prep, a Burbank, California firm that provides tax preparation and accounting services for people in the film and acting industries, offer a comprehensive list of business related tax deductible expenses for your convenience. You can find the list following this section in this chapter. At their website at www.ActorsTaxPrep.com, the expense list is available in a convenient, downloadable PDF version, along with additional helpful information.

Jo's Take

   Recordkeeping is important to both you and the Internal Revenue Service. Follow these basic rules of organization and the job will be a snap.

ActorsTaxPrep.com Expense List

Reprinted with permission

Expense	Expense	Expense
Accounting	Education	Props
Accompanist	Equipment Purchase*	Publicity
Acting Lessons	Film	Real Estate Taxes
Acting Workshops	Film Processing	Registration Auto
Admissions Film	Hairpiece - Wig	Rental Space
Admissions Theater	Hair Styling	Rental Equipment
Advertising	Hotels/Motels	Repairs to Equipment
Agency Fees	Internet Service	Research
Answering Service	Legal Fees	Resumes
Audition Clothes	Licenses	Royalties
Audition Tapes	Manager Fees	Scripts
Books	Medical	Sheet Music
Business Cards	Mortgage Interest	Storage
Business Stationery	Music Arrangements	Student Loan Interest
Business Meals	Music Supplies	Tapes/Audio-Video
Business Entertainment	Office Supplies	Taxi, Bus, Subway
Business Gifts	Pager Service	Tax Preparation
Cellular Phone	Parking fees	Telephone
Charity Cash	Photography	Trade Publications
Charity Other	Photo Reproductions	Travel
Copying	Piano Tuning	Uniforms**
Costumes	Players Directory	Union Dues
Dance Lessons	Portfolio	Vocal Lessons
Demo Reel	Postage/Freight	Websites
Dialect Lessons		

* *Keep track of type of equipment and date purchased.*
** *Uniforms, special clothing and accessories purchased specifically for work assignments.*

16
Soap Operas

Many of today's celebrity performers started their careers as background actors or as actors on television soap operas. This should be a point of great encouragement to you if you dream of moving beyond the world of movie extras.

In the Soaps

Well, my dear readers, I do believe we are about to wrap up this book, which I hope you will find useful in your endeavors to break into an exciting new world. Keep the book with you as a reference guide and remember that I'm holding a good thought for each and every one of you.

More importantly, I hope you'll take my advice and not find yourself in the precarious situations in which I found myself when it came to paying money for unnecessary tools such as acting lessons, photographs, registering with agencies who will never book you and a multitude of ways that could easily make your dreams fade away.

Know that I'm here for you. Again, you'll find me accessible through my website at jkelly4extras.com.

To play on words, here's a little extra "background" about some celebrities who started their careers in the Soaps and went on to the Big Time:

Sarah Michelle Geller, in the starring role of the popular television series, "Buffy the Vampire Slayer," acted in the long-running "All My Children" and was cast for a quickly canceled teen soap opera called "Swan's Crossing."

Russell Crowe, famed for starring roles in "A Beautiful Mind" and "The Insider" was a semi-regular in the long-running Aussie soap opera, "Neighbours."

Bette Midler, who starred in "Gypsy" and "The Stepford Wives," had a short, recurring role in "The Edge of Night."

Christina Applegate of "Married with Children" fame was a regular on the soap opera, "Days of Our Lives."

Julianne Moore, "Laws of Attraction" and "The Hours," acted in the soap operas "The Edge of Night" and "As the World Turns."

Tommy Lee Jones, well known for his role in "Men in Black," "Man of the House" and "Space Cowboys," played Dr. Mark Toland on "One Life to Live."

Lindsay Lohan of "Mean Girls" and "Herbie: Fully Loaded," was well known for her role as Alexandra in "Another World."

Christopher Reeve, famed as "Superman," played Ben Harper on "Love of Life."

Leslie Nielsen, a crack-up in "Airplane," acted on the soap opera, "Peyton Place."

Gates McFadden, who played Dr. Crusher on the highly popular "Star Trek" television series, acted in "All My Children."

Christopher Knight, who was Peter on "The Brady Bunch," paid his dues on the soap called "Another World."

Kevin Bacon of "Footloose" and "Mystic River" fame, worked on "Search for Tomorrow."

Colm Meaney, who endeared himself as Chief Miles O'Brien on "Star Trek: The Next Generation," was briefly a regular on the soap opera, "One Life to Live."

Meg Ryan, known for starring roles in films like "Papa," "Against the Ropes" and "Sleepless in Seattle," performed in "As the World Turns."

Demi Moore, starring in "Charlie's Angels: Full Throttle" and "Ghost," acted in "General Hospital."

Los Angeles Soaps

If you decide to pursue opportunities in the soap opera arena and you live in the Los Angeles area, you're in luck. A number of these popular productions shoot in the Los Angeles area.

All you have to do is submit a photo (I recommend an 8x10 color headshot), and include a resume and your stats with each photo you send. Do not call these companies. If you fit the description of the actor they are seeking, you can count on their calling you.

▣▮▮▮▮▮▣

Days of Our Lives
Attention: Linda Poindexter
Corday Productions
3400 Riverside Drive, #767
Burbank, CA 91505

General Hospital

Attention: Gwen Hillier
ABC Television Center
4151 Prospect Avenue, Stage 54
Los Angeles, CA 90027

Passions

Attention: Don Phillip Smith
Administration Building, #280
4024 Radford Avenue
Studio City, CA 91604

The Bold and the Beautiful

Attention: Christy Dooley, Shannon Bradley
CBS Television City
7800 Beverly Boulevard, #3371
Los Angeles, CA 90036

The Young and the Restless

Attention: Susanne Robbins
CBS Television City
7800 Beverly Boulevard, #3305
Los Angeles, CA 90036

Jo's Take

If you get called and begin working on a soap opera, you'll need to join the American Federation of Television Radio Artists (AFTRA). You needn't seek AFTRA out, as they will come to you and provide all the necessary information when the time is right.

Notes

It's a Wrap

There you have it, my fine thespians. Now, go get them, and remember this:

> *Nothing can take the place of persistence.*
>
> *Talent will not.*
>
> *Nothing is more common than unsuccessful people with talent.*
>
> *Genius will not. Unrewarded genius is almost a proverb.*
>
> *Education will not. The world is full of educated derelicts.*
>
> *Persistence and determination alone are omnipotent. The slogan "Press On" has solved and always will solve the problems of the human race.*
>
> *— Calvin Coolidge*

Reprinted with permission of The Calvin Coolidge Memorial Foundation

Notes

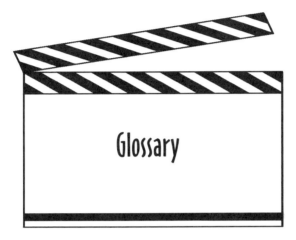

Glossary

Know the Lingo

8x10: A photo showing your head/face; a head shot.

18 to play younger: You'll hear this term a lot on hotlines. This is someone who is legally age eighteeen but could pass for much younger.

Action: This will begin the scene. Actors will begin their dialogue when the Director yells, "Action!" Background actors begin their work when the Director yells "Background."

Actor: Plays a part or role in the scene. The term is used for both male and female roles.

Audition: Acting in a scene for the purpose of showing that you can play the part (to get the job).

AD: Assistant Director to the Director; monitors the filming and its progress.

Agent: Someone who represents the actor to the television or film company and negotiates on your behalf.

Atmosphere: The background actors of the scene.

Back to "One:" Re-set, or start over (also called "From the top.") This means the whole darned shot will be done again and you will return to your starting position and re-do the same scene or take.

Background Actors: "Extras" actors who comprise the "background" of a scene, usually in a non-speaking role.

Base Camp: A location, usually near the set, where background actors, assignments and logistics are coordinated and where background actors meet.

Booking/Booked: Your solid confirmation that you will be working on a set.

Buzz Track: The "natural" or ambient sound associated with a scene, such as the sound of the helicopter hovering over the bad guys, a rushing stream or wind in the trees.

Callback: When you are asked to work another day. Yeah!

Camera Ready: You must show up with your hair and make-up done. Guys, shave and use some deodorant.

Casting Agency: The company working with production studios that books people for background acting assignments.

Casting Director: This is important because this person books you on jobs. You might get a call from Central Casting or Sande Alessi asking your avability for a certain show. That's your casting agency, so write down the name of the person who is booking you.

Cattle Call: A casting call where a large group of people can attend.

Check the Gate: Means they are just going to check the lens for dust and move on to the next shot. A good thing.

Continuity: Most films are shot entirely out of sequence, so filmmakers must be careful that all elements have a logical sequence, backgrounds look the same on Day Two as they did in scenes made on Day One, etc. If you have a two or three day call, expect to wear the same clothes each day, for continuity.

Crosses: The ever so exciting "Action" an Extra makes when the scene is being filmed. If you have ever walked across your living room and back, then you have made crosses. See, extra work can be "exciting!"

Cut: Stop and wait for further instructions.

Cutaway: Shooting of a separate scene, activity or person, which the camera will cut away to show.

Dailies: Unedited film footage from the shoot.

Director: The person in charge of the actors. Your boss.

Double: A performer (could be you) stands in for another performer, usually a lead actor. Also called a "stand-in."

Extra: This is what we are. Background player (or background actor, to be more correct). We are movie extras, and that's a good thing.

Gaffer: Manager of the electrical needs (lighting, etc.) on a shoot.

Golden Time: The magical hour. The sixteenth hour. For example, your call time is 7 am….count sixteen hours and the minute after the sixteenth hour, you are paid your base rate per hour. So if you are making $54 for eight hours, you will be making $54 per hour for every hour over sixteen hours until you are wrapped (released for the day). Yeah!

Grip: People who perform the setup of the set, install the lighting stands, dolly tracks and other equipment.

Headshot: An 8x10 of your face. Your photo should always be a current one (not the one that makes you look ten years younger).

Hiatus: Summer vacation for TV shows; usually from mid-May through August. It's slow, so go take an acting class.

Holding: Where you should be when you are not working on the set. It could be the back of a cold stage or the banquet room of a nice hotel, depending on where your call is. Typically consists of a group of people playing cards, reading or talking about who is casting what. Do some networking.

Honeywagon: This is a huge portable trailer where you'll find a clean bathroom and changing rooms. Not where you'll find food. Sorry.

Hot Set: A set that is currently being used for filming. DON'T TOUCH anything on a hot set EVER.

"In" Time: The actual call time or your start time and also the return time from lunch or dinner.

Location: Where you will be working, i.e., studio, stage or on location, like in a hotel, park or theatre. Usually a natural environment (also see: Set).

Looping: Re-recording an actor's lines in a studio in order to perfectly match them with the action taking place on the screen.

Meal Penalty: Per state law, you must be fed every six hours. If Production does not provide a meal break, then you will be paid an additional fee.

Martini Shot: This will become your favorite phrase. A Martini Shot is the last shot of the day. You'll be wrapped soon and then you can go home, have a Martini, or not.

Mime: Sound is not allowed. No talking, not even a whisper.

Production Company: The organization behind the actual making of the movie or television show.

Rolling: The shooting of a scene is about to begin. The film is rolling in the cameras and the camera is ready to shoot a scene. Another good time to be very quiet.

Scene: The part of the story that is continuous and set in one location or with one actor or group of actors.

Script Doctor: A writer who repairs or customizes the script to make it more workable.

Set: The location of the action being filmed. The set is usually artificially constructed (vs. Location).

Slate: That little chalkboard that displays the scene, title, take number and other important details.

Under-Five: Speaking parts that consist of five lines or less.

Walk-on: A background acting role in which the extra simply walks into or through the scene.

Warm-up: Something you do to prepare your voice and yourself for your role. A serious background actor will consciously get inside the head of his character, no matter how short his crossing or how light his role.

Wear One-Bring Two: Wear an outfit as instructed and bring two similar outfits along with you.

Wrangler: The person charged with managing animals, livestock and sometimes with driving extras.

Wrapped: Finished. You are finished for the day. Get your voucher signed and go home.

Wrecking Crew: A more-or-less "affectionate" term for those who handle the make-up and hair dressing of the actors.

Sources &
Resources

Sources & Resources

Here's a list of books, magazines, organizations and directories you will find useful as you follow your passion to become a good Background Actor or, should you choose to dream beyond, a good Actor.

Academy of Motion Pictures Arts & Sciences – publisher of the Academy Players Directory and home to an extensive library, the Academy also offers special screenings and exhibits. 8949 Wilshire Boulevard, Beverly Hills, CA 90211. Phone 310 247-3000. www.oscars.org.

American Guild of Variety Artists – This is a union representing live variety acts, such as Las Vegas club showroom and cabarets, musical variety shows, comedy showcases, dance revues, magic shows and amusement park shows. AGVA differs from the Equity union in that AGVA shows generally have no storyline. 4741 Laurel Canyon Boulevard, Suite 208, Valley Village, North Hollywood, CA 91607. Phone 818 508-9984.

Back Stage West – Your very own actors trade paper is reachable by phone at 323 525-2356 (editorial), 323 525-2225 (advertising), 323 525-2358 (casting), or 800 745-8922 (subscriber services; call between 5:30 a.m. and 5:30 p.m.). Located at 5055 Wilshire Boulevard, Sixth Floor, Los Angeles, CA 90036.

Central Casting – Central is practically a brand name for casting extras. This agency books the bulk of background actors (extras) for television, films and commercials. The agency takes an upfront photo fee of $20 cash and requires two forms of identification. To help you get more work, they may encourage you to join a fee-based "calling service." 220 South Flower Street, Burbank, CA 91502. Phone 818 562-2755 or visit www.ep-services.com.

Hollywood Global Entertainment Network – networking organization for writers, actors, producers, directors, financiers and others in the film industry. www.hgenonline.com

Screen Actors Guild (SAG) – the union for actors. www.SAG.org

Screen Actors Guild (SAG) Foundation Casting Access Project (CAP) – The fairly new project was very successful in its first year. It connects SAG members with casting professionals in educational workshops, which are free to SAG members. The CAP offers weekly cold reading classes and specialty events including workshops for kids and seniors and sessions for performers with disabilities. Get more details at www.SAGFoundation.org.

The Actors Network – This membership-only organization has the distinction of being the world's only business information, education and resource organization of its kind. It provides invaluable services such as industry guest speakers, topical discussions, member activities and power groups designed to help beginning actors become adept at managing the business side of their performance/artistic careers. For information and/ or to make a reservation for the free orientation, call 818 509-1010 (www.actors-network.com)

The Agencies: What the Actor Needs to Know – This is Lawrence Parker's indispensable guide to Los Angeles agents, agency specialties and the names of agents and their departments in every agency, big and small. It's updated monthly and available for $10 at Hollywood's Samuel French and Take One bookstores.

***The Hollywood Reporter* and *Variety* publications** – These publications are published five days a week. Tuesday's *Reporter* includes complete film production charts, a listing of every project shooting and slated to shoot and often includes contacts for the production companies. *Variety's* TV chart is published on Thursdays; its film chart publishes on Fridays. Visit the web site: www.hollywoodreporter.com; www.variety.com.

The Secret Language of Eating Disorders : How You Can Understand and Work to Cure Anorexia and Bulimia (Vintage), book by Peggy Claude-Pierre. www.Amazon.com

Cutaways

A Letter to the Reader

How this book helps you in your quest to become a good background actor is important to me. I'm interested in learning about your success after reading my book and using my tips.

If you'd like to write me or visit my website, use one of the addresses below:

Best wishes to you,

Jo Kelly
19315 Champion Lane
Huntington Beach, CA 92648

Email: info@jkelly4extras.com
Website: www.JKelly4Extras.com

Index

A

ABC Studios 62
Academy of Motion Pictures
     Arts & Sciences 100
Academy Players Directory
     73, 100
Acting is Everything 73
Acting Schools 38
AFTRA 73
American Guild of
     Variety Artists 100
anorexia 21
Applegate, Christina 85
Atmosphere Talent 28

B

Back Stage West 100
Background Players 11
Background San Diego
     11, 17
Background Talent Services
     28
Bacon, Kevin 85
Bait and Switch 36
Big Boy show 72
Bill Dance Casting 12
business managers 33
Business of Background
     Acting 80
Business of Background
     Acting 79

C

California Governor's
     Committee on
     Employment of People
     with Disabilities 68
California State Labor Code
     36
California state law 43
Calling Services 25
Cameo Casting Services 28
Carpooling 50
Cars, movies 75, 76
Casting Agencies 7, 76
Casting Children 15
CBS Television Center 62
Central Casting 9, 27, 101
Christophere Gray Casting
     18
Corday Productions 12
Crowe, Russell 84
Culver Studios 63
Cutaways 103

D

Days of Our Lives 86
Debe Waisman Casting 12
Disabled, Access 67, 68, 69
Division of Labor Standards
     Enforcement 16

E

Employment Fees 36
Extras 4
Extras Management 27, 29

F

First Day 41, 42
Fox Television Center/KTTV
     63

G

Geller, Sarah Michelle 84
General Hospital 87
Glossary 91
Governor's Committee on
     Employment of People
     with Disabilities 68

H

Hogan, Rich 73, 74
Hollywood Global Entertain-
     ment Network 101
Hollywood Picture Cars 76
Hollywood Reporter 73
Hollywood Talent
     Association 18

I

Internet Come-ons. 38

J

Jeff Olan Casting 13
Johnson, Magic 72
Jones, Tommy Lee 85

K

KBIG 74
Kerr, Judy 73
KFWB 74
Kids Background Talent 18
Kids Hollywood Connection
     18
Knight, Christopher 85
KPWR 74
KRLA 74

L

LA Weekly, 73
Leno, Jay 73
Letter to the Reader 104
licensing, state of California
     33
Lingo 92
Lohan, Lindsay 85
Los Angeles Magazine 73
Los Angeles Tennis Club 51
Los Angeles Times 73

M

Magazines 38
Majestic Studios 63
McFadden, Gates 85
Meaney, Colm 86
Media Access Office 68
Metro Goldwyn Mayer
     (MGM) 63
Midler, Bette 85
Moore, Demi 86
Moore, Julianne 85
Mother-Daughter Story 21
Music Connection 73

N

Nationwide Picture Cars 77
NBC 63
Nielsen, Leslie 85
Notes 110

O

Oceanside Studios 64
On Location Casting 13, 19
On the Set Pointers 45, 46
Order Form 109

P

Paramount Ranch 64
Paramount Studios 64
Passions 87
personal managers 33
Photography 71, 72
Photography Services 37
Picture Vehicles Unlimited 77
Power 106 FM Radio 72
Prime Casting 13, 19
Production Studios 61, 62

R

Raleigh Studios 64
Reeve, Christopher 85
Resources 99, 100
Rich King Casting 14
Riviera, Westminster 77
Ryan, Meg 86

S

Safety Pointers 47
SAG 27, 37, 51, 73
Sande Alessi Casting 11, 17

Screen Actors Guild (SAG)
    5, 53, 54, 101
Screen Children's Casting
    19
Seinfeld 73
Show Mobiles 77
Simmons, Richard 72
Smith & Webster-Davis 14
Soap Operas 83, 84
Soap Operas, Los Angeles
    86
Sony Studios 64
South Bay Studios 65
Specialty Vehicle Association
    76
State Approval 38
Studio Kids Management 20
Sunset Casting 72, 74
Sunset Gower Studios 65
Sunset Stage 65

T

Talent Agencies 31, 32
The Actors Network 101
The Agencies: What the
    Actor Needs to Know
    102
The Bold and the Beautiful
    86, 87
The Hollywood Reporter
    102
The Lot 65
The Making of a Headshot
    73
The Young and the Restless
    87

Time Warner 73
Tina Real Casting 14
Tonight Show 73
Turner, Tina 72
Twentieth Century Fox 65

U

Universal Studios/MCA 65

V

Valencia Studios 65
Variety 73, 102

W

Walt Disney Studios 66
Wardrobe 57, 58
Warner Brothers Studios 66
Warner Hollywood Studios
    66
Warner Ranch 66
Work Permit 16
World TV Productions 66

Order Form

How to Become a Good Background Actor

Name _____

Shipping Address _____

_____

City _____

State/Province _____

Country _____

Zip/Postal Code _____

Telephone (_____) _____

Quantity

___ books at $18.95 US = $_____

___ books at $22.95 Canada = $_____

California residents, please add
7.75% state sales tax = $_____

Shipping

    1 book = $3.00 $_____
    2 books = $4.00 $_____
    3 books = $5.00 $_____

Total: $_____

Make CHECK Payable To:
Background Actors Seminars
19315 Champion Lane
Huntington Beach, CA 92648

Notes

Notes